Leach Library
276 Mammoth Road
Londonderry, NH 03053
Adult Services 432-1132
Children's Services 432-1127

Ben Roethlisberger

By Jeffrey Zuehlke

AMAZING ATHLETES

Lerner Publications Company • Minneapolis

J
BIO
ROT

08·4·23
WAG 2249

For Big Uncle Ben

Lerner Publications Company
A division of Lerner Publishing Group, Inc.
241 First Avenue North
Minneapolis, MN 55401 U.S.A.

Website address: www.lernerbooks.com

Library of Congress Cataloging-in-Publication Data

Zuehlke, Jeffrey, 1968–
        Ben Roethlisberger / by Jeffrey Zuehlke.
            p.   cm. — (Amazing athletes)
        Includes index.
        ISBN-13: 978-0-8225-7660-0 (lib. bdg. : alk. paper)
        1. Roethlisberger, Ben, 1982–Juvenile literature. 2. Football players—United States—Biography—Juvenile literature. 3. Roethlisberger, Ben, 1982– 4. Football players—United States—Biography. I. Title.
        GV939.R64Z84 2008
        796.332092—dc22 [B]   2006100582

Manufactured in the United States of America
1 2 3 4 5 6 — DP — 13 12 11 10 09 08

TABLE OF CONTENTS

Ben sets his feet to throw a long pass in Super Bowl XL (40) against the Seattle Seahawks.

Big-Game Ben

Ben Roethlisberger took the **snap**. The Pittsburgh Steelers' **quarterback** dropped back to pass. The Steelers were trailing 3–0 to the Seattle Seahawks in **Super Bowl** XL. Worse yet, it was third **down** and 28. The Steelers needed to get 28 yards to have a chance to score.

The Seahawks' **pass rush** came hard and fast. Ben calmly scanned the field for an open receiver. Seattle's Grant Wistrom ran straight toward Ben. But Ben's quick feet helped him get away. Wistrom kept coming after him.

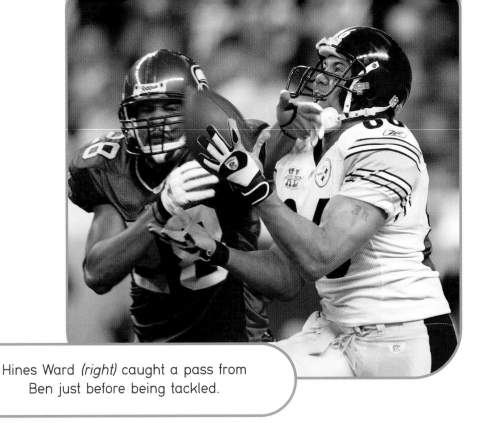

Hines Ward *(right)* caught a pass from Ben just before being tackled.

Pittsburgh's star quarterback looked downfield. He set his feet and launched a long pass across the field. Steelers' **wide receiver** Hines Ward snatched it at the three-yard line. He was tackled instantly. The Steelers had a first down!

On first and second down, the Steelers couldn't get the ball in the **end zone**. Coach Bill Cowher decided to give his big, strong quarterback a shot. Ben took the snap. Steelers' **running back** Jerome Bettis threw a powerful block. Following his teammate, Ben dove into the end zone. **Touchdown**! After kicking the extra point, the Steelers took the lead, 7–3.

The two teams kept slugging it out. The Steelers went into the fourth quarter with a slim 14–10 lead. Cowher called a trick play. Ben flipped the ball to running back Willie Parker. Parker handed it off to his speedy teammate, Antwaan Randle El.

Randle El got ready to pass the ball. Hines Ward was wide open downfield! But Seattle **safety** Michael Boulware had broken through the Steelers' line. The hard-hitting Boulware zeroed in on Randle El.

Ben wears number 7 in honor of former Denver Broncos star quarterback, John Elway.

Would Boulware break up the play? Suddenly, Ben threw himself in front of Boulware. The Steelers quarterback knocked Boulware aside. Randle El delivered a perfect throw to Ward. Touchdown!

Pittsburgh held on to win the game, 21–10. Ben and the Steelers were Super Bowl champions! The twenty-three-year-old had become the youngest quarterback ever to win a Super Bowl.

Ben raises the Vince Lombardi trophy after the Steelers' triumph in Super Bowl XL.

Ben's family eventually moved to Findlay, Ohio. He played football at Findlay High School. Here, Ben tries to throw a pass before getting sacked.

STAR ATHLETE

Ben Roethlisberger was born March 2, 1982, in Lima, Ohio. Ben's childhood wasn't easy. His parents divorced when he was two years old. Ben's mom was killed in a car accident when he was eight.

In 1999, Ben was the team captain (leader) of Findlay's football, baseball, and basketball teams. He had a .300 batting average in baseball. He scored more than 26 points per game in basketball.

Ben grew up in Findlay, a small city in northwestern Ohio. He lived with his dad, Ken, his stepmom, Brenda, and his younger sister, Carlee.

Ben was a natural athlete. He was especially good at basketball and football. "He has a lot of God-given talent and natural ability," said his fifth-grade football coach.

At Findlay High School, Ben was a star athlete. He became the school's all-time leading scorer in basketball. He was a star shortstop on the baseball team. Ben was also a talented quarterback. In 1999, as a senior, Ben had a huge year. He threw for 4,041 yards. He also completed 54 touchdown passes. He was named Ohio's Division I Offensive Player of the Year. By this time, colleges were offering Ben **scholarships**. He chose to play for the RedHawks at Miami University in Ohio.

Ben played at Findlay High School. He greets his former football coach Cliff Hite during a game.

Ben dives for a first down in a game against the University of North Carolina Tar Heels.

RedHawks Rule!

Ben didn't play in 2000, his first year at Miami. But he earned the starting quarterback job in 2001. He soon caught people's attention with his strong arm. One of his best moments came in a game against the University of Akron. In the fourth quarter, the RedHawks were trailing. Ben cut loose a long 70-yard touchdown pass that won the game.

Ben finished his first season with 25 touchdown passes. He threw for 3,105 yards. Outstanding! His 2002 season was nearly as good. Ben threw for 3,238 yards and 22 touchdowns.

By 2003, his third year of playing in college, NFL **scouts** were giving Ben high marks. They loved his size and powerful arm. Scouts also liked Ben's personality. He was smart, hard-working, and humble.

Ben's skill at throwing long passes attracted NFL scouts.

When people praised him, he didn't let it go to his head. Instead, he made sure his teammates shared the credit for his success. The RedHawks won 12 games in a row in 2003. Magazines such as *Sports Illustrated* and the *Sporting News* published articles about Ben.

Many people felt he was good enough to play in the NFL. Would he skip his last year of college and turn pro? But Ben refused to talk about his future plans. "I'm having too much fun right now to think about that," he said.

The Miami University RedHawks play in the Mid-American Conference (MAC). The schools in the conference are located in the Midwest. Other MAC schools include the University of Akron and Bowling Green State University. Ben had memorable games against both schools.

In December 2003, the RedHawks battled the Falcons of Bowling Green State University. The two teams were playing in the Mid-American Conference (MAC) Championship Game. Ben threw for an incredible 440 yards with four touchdowns. The RedHawks clobbered the Falcons 49–27.

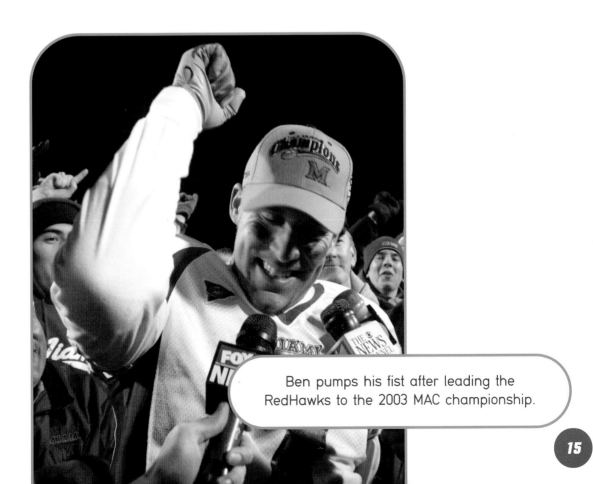

Ben pumps his fist after leading the RedHawks to the 2003 MAC championship.

The win was Miami's first MAC championship since 1986. The RedHawks finished their season by beating up Louisville 49–28 in the GMAC Bowl.

Ben's amazing season was complete. He decided to skip his last year at Miami and enter the 2004 NFL **draft**. In April 2004, the Pittsburgh Steelers selected him with the 11th pick.

Ben shows off a Pittsburgh Steelers' jersey at the NFL draft in New York in 2004.

JUMPING IN

Most NFL quarterbacks don't play much during their first year. Instead, they spend the season on the **sidelines**. They watch, listen, study, and learn.

When **training camp** started, Steelers coach Bill Cowher named Ben the **third-string** quarterback. Tommy Maddox was the starter. Charlie Batch was the backup. But then Batch hurt his knee. Ben became the backup.

Maddox injured his elbow during the second game of the season. Suddenly, Ben was the starting quarterback. He was under a lot of pressure.

At training camp, Ben practiced hard. He learned how to work with his new team.

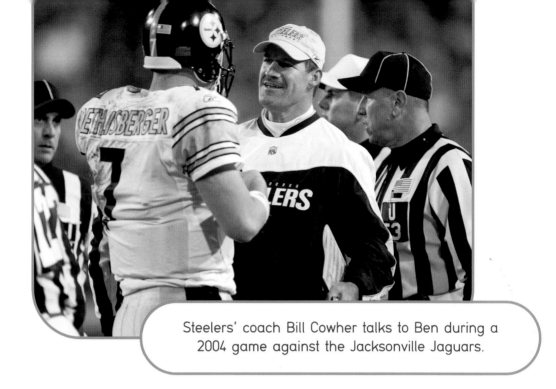

Steelers' coach Bill Cowher talks to Ben during a 2004 game against the Jacksonville Jaguars.

Luckily, he had a lot of great **veteran** players on his team. They included Jerome Bettis and Hines Ward. And the Steelers had one of the toughest defenses in the NFL. Ben wouldn't have to win games all by himself.

Ben's first start came against the Miami Dolphins. In the fourth quarter, he threw a touchdown pass to seal the win, 13–3. Wins over the Cincinnati Bengals, the Cleveland Browns, and the Dallas Cowboys followed.

Ben waves to Steelers' fans after a win over the Philadelphia Eagles.

Ben and the Steelers were on a roll. Everyone praised Ben's smarts. They also noted his leadership skills. "He has come a long way and fast," said teammate Jeff Hastings.

The Steelers' winning streak continued. In November, they beat two of the NFL's best teams—the New England Patriots and the Philadelphia Eagles. Pittsburgh looked unstoppable. Could Ben be the first rookie quarterback to win the Super Bowl?

Pittsburgh finished the 2004 regular season

with 15 wins and just 1 loss. They went on to win their first **playoff** game. This win set up a rematch with New England. The teams played in the **American Football Conference (AFC) Championship Game**.

The Steelers finally met their match. Patriots' quarterback Tom Brady picked apart the Steelers' defense. Ben threw three interceptions. The Steelers lost, 41–27. The loss was tough, but Steelers' fans had plenty to be excited about.

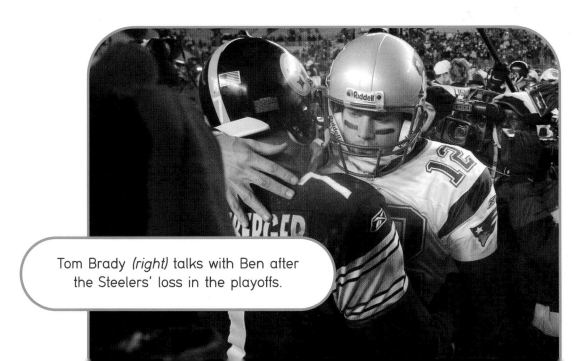

Tom Brady *(right)* talks with Ben after the Steelers' loss in the playoffs.

Ben is helped off the field after a knee injury. The Steelers went on to beat the San Diego Chargers.

YOUNG CHAMPION

The Steelers enjoyed a strong start in 2005. They won their first two games. But Ben missed some games with a knee injury. Jerome Bettis and Hines Ward also struggled with injuries. The Steelers found it hard to win without their best players.

After 12 games, Pittsburgh had just 7 wins and 5 losses. They might miss the playoffs. To keep their Super Bowl dreams alive, the Steelers had to win the final four **regular season** games.

Ben and his teammates stepped up. They reeled off four wins in a row. Their strong finish earned them a playoff spot. But the Super Bowl was three wins away. To get there, the Steelers would have to win three games on the road. They started the playoffs in Cincinnati, Ohio. Ben threw three touchdown passes to defeat the Bengals, 31–21.

Ben is very popular in Pittsburgh. A restaurant sells a sandwich named after him. The Roethlis-burger is made with hamburger, sausage, scrambled eggs, and American cheese. It sells for $7—Ben's jersey number.

A week later, the Steelers traveled to Indianapolis, Indiana. They'd face the high-powered Indianapolis Colts. But Pittsburgh's defense roughed up Colts' star quarterback, Peyton Manning. And Ben threw two touchdown passes.

With less than two minutes left, the Steelers had the lead, 21–18. One more touchdown would make sure they'd win the game. Ben handed off the ball to Bettis. He plowed toward the end zone. A Colts' player hit Bettis hard. The ball flew out of his hands. **Fumble**!

Another Colts' **defender**, Nick Harper, picked up the ball. He sprinted toward the Steelers' end zone. A Colts' touchdown would give them the lead! Ben was the only Pittsburgh player who had a chance to tackle him. Ben dove at Harper and grabbed his leg. The Colts' defender tripped and fell. Ben had stopped the score! The Steelers held on to win.

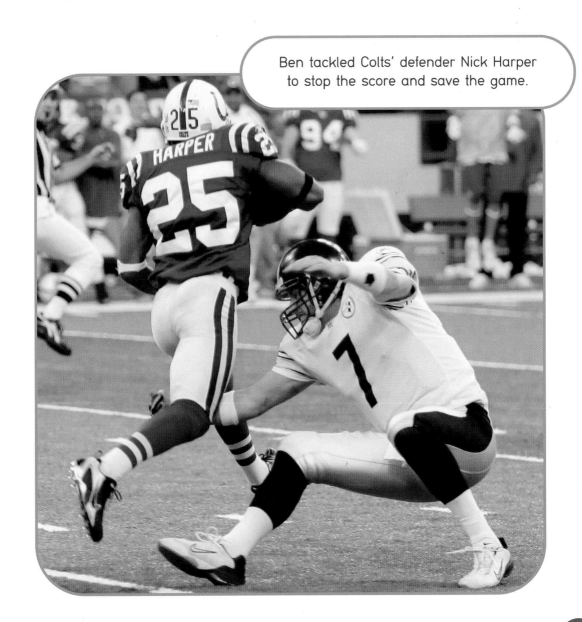

Ben tackled Colts' defender Nick Harper to stop the score and save the game.

Reporters surround Ben after the Steelers' win over the Denver Broncos.

The Steelers' final road game was in Denver, Colorado, against the Broncos. Denver couldn't stop the Steelers. Ben threw two touchdown passes and ran for a third touchdown. The Steelers won, 34–17.

Getting to Super Bowl XL had been amazing. Winning it was even sweeter! Ben became one of the NFL's most popular players. He appeared on TV talk shows. Wherever he went, fans congratulated him.

Ben's fun came to a scary end in June 2006. He was enjoying riding his motorcycle, when he crashed with a car. Ben wasn't wearing a helmet. His head hit the car's windshield. Ben suffered serious injuries.

Ben's injuries healed quickly. He looked set to start the 2006 regular season. But he became ill. He had to have surgery to remove his appendix. He missed the first few games of the season.

Pittsburgh police officers look at Ben's wrecked motorcycle.

Ben gets sacked during a 2006 game against the Jacksonville Jaguars. The Steelers lost the game, 9–0.

When Ben finally came back, he struggled. The team was unable to score at all in two games. They lost close games as well. Even though the 2006 season wasn't successful, Ben is committed to improving. Steelers' fans still have high hopes for the future with Big Ben leading the team.

Selected Career Highlights

2006   Became youngest quarterback to win a Super Bowl

2005   Threw for 2,385 yards and 17 touchdowns

2004   Threw for 2,621 yards and 17 touchdowns
Named NFL Offensive Rookie of the Year
Led Steelers to 15 straight regular season wins
Drafted by the Pittsburgh Steelers with the 11th pick
   in the first round

2003   Led Miami RedHawks to 49–28 win over the Louisville
   Cardinals in the GMAC Bowl
Threw for 440 yards and 4 touchdowns to win 49–27
   over the Bowling Green Falcons in the MAC championship
Threw for 4,486 yards and 37 touchdowns in 14 games
Named third-team All-American

2002   Threw for 3,238 yards and 22 touchdowns
Led RedHawks to 7 wins and 5 losses

2001   Threw for 3,105 yards and 25 touchdowns
Led RedHawks to 7 wins and 5 losses

1999   Passed for 4,041 yards in his senior year at Findlay High School
Threw 54 touchdown passes
Named Ohio's Division I Offensive Player of the Year

Glossary

American Football Conference (AFC) Championship Game: a playoff game in which the two top teams in the American Football Conference play to decide who will go to the Super Bowl

defender: a player whose job it is to stop the other team from scoring

down: one of four chances a team has to move the football 10 yards

draft: an event where sports teams choose players

end zone: the area beyond the goal line at each end of the field. A team scores six points when it reaches the other team's end zone.

fumble: to lose hold of the football

pass rush: a play where the defensive players run toward the quarterback to keep him from throwing a pass

playoff: one of a series of games held every year to decide the NFL champion

quarterback: a player whose main job is to throw passes

regular season: the regular schedule for a season. In the NFL, each team plays 16 games. The top 12 teams go to the playoffs.

running back: an offensive player whose main job is to run with the ball

safety: a defensive player whose main job is to stop passes to wide receivers

scholarships: money awarded to students to pay for the cost of attending college

scouts: persons who judge an athlete's skills

sidelines: the area to the side of the field of play

snap: an action in which the offensive team's center gives the ball to the quarterback

Super Bowl: the NFL's championship game

third-string: third in line for the starter's job

touchdown: a six-point score. A team scores a touchdown when it gets into the other team's end zone with the ball.

training camp: a period during the summer when a team gets ready for the season

veteran: a player with several years of experience

wide receiver: an offensive player whose main job is to catch passes

Further Reading & Websites

Rappoport, Ken. *Jerome Bettis*. Berkeley Heights, NJ: Enslow Elementary, 2003.

Savage, Jeff. *Play-by-Play Football*. Minneapolis: Lerner Publications Company, 2003.

Stewart, Mark. *The Pittsburgh Steelers*. Chicago: Norwood House Press, 2007.

Ben Roethlisberger Official Site
http://www.br-7.com/
Visit Ben's official website to see pictures of Ben and to learn all about his exciting life in the NFL.

Espn.com
http://espn.com
Espn.com covers all the major professional sports, including the National Football League.

NFL.com
http://www.nfl.com
The official site of the National Football League provides up-to-date news and statistics of all 32 NFL teams, including the Pittsburgh Steelers.

Official Pittsburgh Steelers site
http://www.steelers.com
The official website of the Pittsburgh Steelers has team news, stats, scores, statistics, and more.

Sports Illustrated for Kids
http://www.sikids.com
The *Sports Illustrated for Kids* website covers all sports, including football.

Super Bowl History
http://www.superbowl.com/history
Visit the NFL's official Super Bowl site to read about and see pictures and video of every Super Bowl.

Index

Photo Acknowledgments

The images in this book are used with the permission of: © Jonathan Ferrey/Getty Images, pp. 4, 6; © Jeff Haynes/AFP/Getty Images, p. 8; © Mark Deckard, p. 9; AP Photo/The Courier, Howard Moyer, p. 11; AP Photo/Grant Halverson, p. 12; AP Photo/Dave Martin, p. 13; AP Photo/Daniel Miller, p. 15; © Chris Trotman/Getty Images, p. 17; © Jason Cohn/Icon SMI, p. 18; © Grant Halverson/Getty Images, p. 19; © Harry How/Getty Images, p. 20; © Jay Drowns/Sporting News/ZUMA Press, p. 21; © Tom Hauck/Getty Images, p. 22; AP Photo/Michael Conroy, p. 25; © Jonathan Daniel/Getty Images, p. 26; AP Photo/Pittsburgh Tribune-Review, Philip G. Pavely, p. 27; © Marc Serota/Getty Images, p. 28; © Larry French/Getty Images, p. 29.

Front Cover: © Rick Stewart/Getty Images.